MACMILLAN READERS

PRE-INTERMEDIATE LEVEL

MEG CABOT

The
Princess Diaries 3

Retold by Anne Collins

PRE-INTERMEDIATE LEVEL

Founding Editor: John Milne

The Macmillan Readers provide a choice of enjoyable reading materials for learners of English. The series is published at six levels – Starter, Beginner, Elementary, Pre-intermediate, Intermediate and Upper.

Level control
Information, structure and vocabulary are controlled to suit the students' ability at each level.

The number of words at each level:

Starter	about 300 basic words
Beginner	about 600 basic words
Elementary	about 1100 basic words
Pre-intermediate	about 1400 basic words
Intermediate	about 1600 basic words
Upper	about 2200 basic words

Vocabulary
Some difficult words and phrases in this book are important for understanding the story. Some of these words are explained in the story and some are shown in the pictures. From Pre-intermediate level upwards, words are marked with a number like this: ...[3]. These words are explained in the Glossary at the end of the book.

Answer keys
Answer keys for the *Points for Understanding* and the *Exercises* sections can be found at www.macmillanenglish.com

Contents

A Note About the Author and This Story

Meg Cabot (Meggin Patricia Cabot) was born in Bloomington, Indiana, U.S.A. She lives in New York City with her husband, Benjamin, and her cat, Henrietta. Meg Cabot studied Art at Indiana University. Then she became an illustrator of books and magazines.

Meg's first novel, *Where Roses Grow Wild*, was published in 1988. She wrote this book using the name Patricia Cabot. Her favorite authors are Jane Austen, Judy Blume, and Barbara Cartland. Her favorite food is pizza.

Some of Meg Cabot's stories are: *The Princess Diaries* (2000), *The Princess Diaries: Take Two* (2000), *The Princess Diaries: Third Time Lucky* (2001), *The Princess Diaires: Mia Goes Forth* (2002), *The Princess Diaries: Give Me Five* (2003). *The Princess Diaries* series has been made into two movies – *The Princess Diaries* and *The Princess Diaries 2: Royal Engagement* (Buena Vista/Walt Disney Pictures, 2001/ 2004).

email a way of sending messages from one computer to another.

chatrooms you can have a conversation in an Internet chatroom.

online using a computer to talk to people on a computer network, and to search for information on the Internet.

Instant Message communicating with someone directly over the Internet and replying to their messages as soon as they arrive.

text message a written message that you send or receive using a mobile phone.

The People in This Story

Grandmere (Clarisse Marie Renaldo)

Philippe Renaldo

Helen Thermopolis

Frank Gianini

Mia (Amelia) Thermopolis Fat Louie

Doctor Moscovitz

Doctor Moscovitz

Lilly Moscovitz

Michael Moscovitz

Sebastiano
Grimaldi

Boris Pelkowski

Tina Hakim Baba

Josh Richter

Lana Weinberger

Principal Gupta

Lars

Wahim

Shameeka Taylor

Kenny Showalter

Dave Farouq
El-Abar

1

A Girl with Two Lives

My name is Mia Thermopolis. A few months ago, my mom gave me this diary because she wanted me to write down my feelings. Now I write about everything that happens to me.

I go to the Albert Einstein High School in New York City. I'm fourteen years old and I used to be an ordinary schoolgirl. But now my life isn't ordinary at all.

I live in an apartment in Greenwich Village, on the west side of the city. I live with my mom, Helen, and my cat, Fat Louie. My mom is an artist and she's beautiful. Last month she got married to Mr Gianini, my Algebra[1] teacher at school. So now Mr Gianini is my new stepfather[2] and he lives with us too.

My mom is three months pregnant[3]. So I'm going to have a new baby half-brother or half-sister. I'm very happy about this.

I'm a freshman—a ninth grade student—at Albert Einstein High School. My best friend is Lilly Moscovitz. I have other school friends too, like Tina Hakim Baba and Shameeka Taylor. My worst subject at school is Algebra. I keep flunking Algebra—I fail every test—so I have to go to Mr Gianini's extra Algebra classes.

Two months ago, I had a big shock. My dad, Philippe Renaldo, came to New York and told me that I'm the Princess of Genovia. Genovia is a small country in Europe, near the border of France and Italy. My full name is Her Royal Highness Princess Amelia Mignonette Grimaldi Thermopolis Renaldo. My dad is the Prince of Genovia.

My mom and dad weren't married when I was born. My mom didn't want to marry my dad so she became a single parent. But although my mom and dad weren't in love with each other, they stayed friends. When I was growing up, my dad sent us money. And every summer I visited him in Genovia.

But then everything changed. My dad got cancer[4]. He had an operation and the doctors cut the cancer out of his body. Then he had chemotherapy[5]. The chemotherapy worked well but now my dad is sterile—he can't have any more children. So I'm my dad's heir[6]. When he dies, I'll become the ruler of Genovia.

My dad's mother—Grandmere—is the Dowager[7] Princess of Genovia. Grandmere speaks French, drinks cocktails[8] and smokes a lot of cigarettes. Many people are frightened of her. She's staying in a suite of rooms at the Plaza Hotel in New York. Every day after school, Grandmere gives me princess lessons.

So I have two lives—a life as an ordinary schoolgirl, and a life as a princess.

_____

My English teacher told our class to write about what our family did on Thanksgiving Day[9].

I had two different kinds of Thanksgiving Day dinners, so I wrote about both of them.

My Thanksgiving by Mia Thermopolis

6:45 a.m. I was woken up by the sound of my mother being sick. She is three months pregnant so she is sick every morning.

7:45 a.m. Mr Gianini, my new stepfather, knocks on my door. He says that it's time to get up. Mr Gianini, my mom and I are having Thanksgiving dinner at his parents' house on Long Island. The roads will be very busy because everyone is going to visit their families. Mr Gianini says that we have to leave now if we want to miss the traffic.

8:45 a.m. There is no traffic at this time in the morning on Thanksgiving Day. So we arrive at Mr Gianini's house three hours early.

12:00. Mr Gianini's sister arrives with her husband and their daughter, Claire. Claire is my age but I know we aren't going to like each other. Claire looks at me.

'YOU'RE the one who's supposed to be a princess?" she says.

1:00 p.m. The food is served. We begin eating.

1:15 p.m. We finish eating.

1:20 p.m. I help Mr Gianini's mother clean up in the kitchen. She tells me to go and chat with Claire. But I don't want to talk to Claire.

3:00 p.m. We leave because we have to get home before the traffic gets bad. I say goodbye, but Claire doesn't say goodbye to me.

6:30 p.m. We arrive home late. There were a lot of cars on the road. I just have time to change into a long blue evening dress and a pair of flat blue shoes. Then Lars, my bodyguard, arrives to take me to my second Thanksgiving dinner at the Plaza Hotel. Lars' job is to look after me because I am the Princess of Genovia. He must stop anyone from trying to kidnap[10] me.

7:30 p.m. We arrive at the Plaza Hotel. My father, the Prince of Genovia, and his mother, the Dowager Princess, have rented the Palm Court dining room for the evening. They are having a Thanksgiving party. Grandmere has invited about two hundred of her closest friends. Her guests include the Emperor[11] of Japan and his wife.

That's why I have to wear flat shoes. Grandmere says it's rude to be taller than an emperor.

11:30 p.m. I am very tired because I had to get up so early this morning. At last, my father allows me to leave and Lars drives me back to the apartment.

12:00 a.m. After a long and tiring day, I finally go to bed.

And that's the end of Mia Thermopolis's Thanksgiving.

Saturday, December 5th

My life is over. O–V–E–R.

I know I have said this before, but this time I really mean it.

And why is my life over? Because I have a *boyfriend*.

All my friends have boyfriends. Even my friend Lilly has one. Lilly's boyfriend is Boris Pelkowski. He's fifteen years old and he's a very good musician. He also wears weird clothes.

When Lilly got a boyfriend, I got worried because I didn't have one. I thought there must be something wrong with me.

And then one day, I got a boyfriend too.

A boy named Kenny from my Biology class started sending me anonymous[12] love letters. Kenny didn't sign his name so I didn't know they were from him. I was hoping they were from Lilly's older brother Michael. I've been in love with Michael for a long time, but he doesn't know how I feel. He just sees me as his kid sister's friend.

So when Kenny said that he had sent me the love letters, I didn't know what to do. I like Kenny, but only as a friend.

There's a big dance at school at the end of this semester—the Albert Einstein Winter Dance. I'm going to the dance with Kenny. Well, he hasn't asked me yet, but he will. He has to ask me because he's my boyfriend.

I must be the luckiest girl in the world. I'm not pretty, but I'm not ugly, I live in New York and I'm a princess. I have a boyfriend. What more could a girl ask for?

It's no good. The truth is: I DON'T EVEN LIKE KENNY.

Kenny is a nice guy. But when I see him, my heart doesn't start beating faster. And when Kenny holds my hand or kisses me, it's not exciting at all.

Sometimes, when Kenny tries to kiss me, I turn my head away.

I know I have to break up[13] with Kenny. I must tell him that I only like him as a friend. But I don't want to upset him.

And there's another problem. On Saturday nights, Kenny and I go out with Lilly and her boyfriend, Boris. Sometimes we are joined by my friends, Tina Hakim Baba and her boyfriend, Dave Farouq El-Abar, and my other friend Shameeka Taylor, and her boyfriend, Daryl Gardner. So we are four couples—Lilly-and-Boris, Kenny-and-Mia, Tina-and-Dave and Shameeka-and-Daryl.

So if Kenny and I break up, who will I go out with on Saturday evenings? And who will take me to the Winter Dance?

2

Michael and Judith

Saturday, December 5th, 11:00 p.m.

My life has just got worse.

Last night, Lilly-and-Boris and Tina-and-Dave and Mia-and-Kenny went ice-skating. We were joined by a new couple, Michael-and-Judith. Lilly's brother Michael brought Judith Gershner to the ice-rink[14].

I'm not surprised that Michael likes Judith. Judith is the President of the Computer Club. Judith, like Michael, is a senior student. Judith, like Michael, is very smart and is going to college in the fall. Judith, like Michael, won a prize last year at school for her science project[15]. She cloned[16] a fruit fly. In her bedroom at home.

When I saw Judith and Michael together, I got a terrible feeling inside. I felt very jealous of Judith.

"Look, there's your brother," I said to Lilly. "I didn't know your brother and Judith Gershner were going out."

Lilly doesn't know that I'm in love with Michael.

"They're not," said Lilly. "Judith was at our place. She was working with Michael on a project for the Computer Club. I told them that we were going skating, and Judith said she wanted to come too."

I watched Michael and Judith skating. Michael could skate very well but Judith wasn't very good. She was holding on to Michael's hands as they skated.

I don't know how to clone a fruit fly, but I do know how to skate better than Judith.

Then Kenny came up. He wanted to skate with me like Michael was skating with Judith. So Kenny took my hands and tried to pull me around the ice rink.

"I know how to skate, Kenny," I said.

But Kenny wouldn't go away. So finally, I let him hold my hands as he skated in front of me.

But it was difficult to skate with Kenny skating in front of me. He fell down and I couldn't stop, so I crashed into him. My chin hit his knee and I bit my tongue. I could feel my mouth filling up with blood. Everyone around the ice-rink was staring at me. I felt really stupid and embarrassed.

Now I'm here at home in bed with only my cat, Fat Louie, beside me. My tongue hurts and I can't talk. And the boy I love is with another girl. A girl who is much smarter than me.

Sunday, December 6th
I've just got back from dinner at Grandmere's.

I have to go to Genovia at the end of December. On Christmas Eve[17] my dad will make a speech on Genovian national television. He's going to introduce me to the Genovian people. I'm very nervous about appearing on Genovian TV in front of 50,000 people.

My cousin, Sebastiano Grimaldi, was also at dinner. Grandmere brought Sebastiano to New York because he is a fashion designer[18]. Sebastiano is going to design the dress I will wear for my TV appearance.

Sebastiano is about thirty, with long dark hair which he ties back. He is very tall and he wears brightly-colored clothes. Tonight he was wearing a blue velvet[19] jacket with leather trousers. He speaks English with a French accent and he says only the first syllable of English words. He says "nar" instead of "narrow"; "cof" instead "of "coffee" and "madge" instead of "magical". It's very funny.

I want Sebastiano to design a really nice dress for me. I want a dress that will make Michael Moscovitz forget about Judith Gershner. I want a dress that will make him think only about me, Mia Thermopolis.

After dinner, Sebastiano drew a design for the dress. Grandmere looked at his drawing.

"That's brilliant. Just brilliant," she said.

I looked at the design. The dress looked very ordinary.

"Um," I said. "Can't you make it a little more . . . sexy?"

Grandmere and Sebastiano looked at each other.

"Sexy?" said Grandmere in a surprised voice. Then they both began to laugh.

While they were laughing, my dad got up and left the table. He went outside to the balcony. Grandmere and Sebastiano were still talking so I went outside and joined my dad.

"Mia," he said when he saw me. "What are you doing out here? It's cold. Go back inside."

"I will in a minute," I said. I stood next to him and looked out over New York. From the Plaza Hotel, there is a wonderful view of Manhattan—the island in the center of New York. You can see the lights in all the windows.

Suddenly, I realized[15] that one of those lights probably belonged to Judith Gershner. Then I felt very sad. My dad looked at me and noticed that something was wrong.

"Look, I know that Sebastiano is a difficult person," he said. "But he's only here for a couple of weeks."

"I wasn't thinking about Sebastiano," I said sadly.

I don't usually tell my dad about my problems with my love life. But my dad has had a lot of girlfriends so I thought perhaps he could give me some good advice.

"Dad," I said. "What do you do if you like someone—but they don't know that you like them?"

"I'm sure Kenny knows that you like him," said my dad. "You go out with him every weekend."

"I'm not talking about Kenny, Dad," I said. "Kenny and I are just friends. I'm talking about Lilly's brother, Michael."

My dad looked very surprised.

I stood next to my dad and looked out over New York.

"Isn't Michael in college?" he said.

"Not yet," I replied. "He's going to college in the fall."

Then my dad looked worried.

"Don't worry, Dad," I said. "Michael would never be interested in a girl like me."

"What do you mean?" my dad asked in an annoyed voice. "What's wrong with you?"

"Dad," I said. "I almost flunked Algebra, remember? Michael is very smart."

"You may not be good at Algebra," said my dad, "but you and I, Mia, are intelligent people." Then he said, "Don't make the same mistake as me. Don't keep your feelings to yourself because you are too shy . . . or too proud, to tell the person you love how you feel."

I looked at my dad in surprise. He sounded so . . . *sad*. Was he talking about Mom? But Mom would never be happy living in Genovia. She likes living in New York. She likes American TV and American food.

"What do you think I should do, Dad?" I asked. "Do you think I should tell Michael that I like him?"

My dad shook his head.

"No, no, no," he said. "You have to tell him by *showing* him how you feel."

"Oh," I said. I didn't really know what my dad was talking about.

My mom has just come into my room to say that Kenny is on the phone for me.

I suppose Kenny wants to ask me to the Winter Dance.

Sunday, December 6th, 11:00 p.m.

I am very shocked. Kenny did NOT ask me to the Winter Dance. Instead, this was our conversation:

ME: Hello?

KENNY: Hi, Mia. It's Kenny.

ME: Oh, hi Kenny. What's the matter?

Kenny sounded strange, which is why I asked.

KENNY: Well, I just wanted to see if you were OK. I mean, if your tongue is OK.

ME: It's a little better.

KENNY: Because I was really worried. You know, I really didn't mean to pull you down like that.

ME: Kenny, I know. It was just an accident.

KENNY: Well, I just wanted to say that I hope you feel better. And also to let you know . . . well, Mia, that I love you.

I was SO shocked!! What kind of guy calls a girl on the phone and says I love you??? Why is Kenny telling me this?

Kenny was still on the phone, waiting.

ME: Um, OK.

Poor Kenny. I know he wanted a different kind of answer. But I didn't know what else to say. So I said,

ME: Well, see you tomorrow.

AND I HUNG UP THE PHONE!!!!

I really am the most terrible, ungrateful[21] girl in the world.

3

Talking with Tina

Monday, December 7th. Homeroom[22]

Every morning, Lars drives me to school and we pick up Lilly and Michael. But this morning, Michael wasn't there because he had a dentist appointment. So while we were in the car, I told Lilly about Kenny. I told her that he called and said he loved me.

Lilly didn't believe me.

"Kenny would never say that," she said. "He probably said something else and you didn't hear him properly."

"Oh?" I said. "What could Kenny have said that sounded like I love you? *I glove you?*"

Then Lilly got mad.

"No, of course not. You know, you have been behaving strangely about Kenny. You used to say, 'Why don't I have a boyfriend? When am I going to get a boyfriend?' And now you have one, you're not even grateful."

I knew that this was true. But I didn't want to admit it.

"That's not true," I replied. "I'm very grateful about Kenny."

"Really?" said Lilly. "Mia, I think that you're not ready to have a boyfriend."

Now I was really mad.

"Me? Not ready to have a boyfriend? I've been waiting my whole life to have a boyfriend!"

"So why won't you let him kiss you on the lips?" asked Lilly.

"Where did you hear that?" I asked.

"Kenny told Boris, of course. And Boris told me."

I was very shocked but I tried to stay calm.

"That's *great*," I said. "So now our boyfriends are talking about us?"

"Mia," said Lilly, "If Kenny did say 'the L word'—you know, '*Love*'—it was because you won't let him show you how he feels. You won't let him kiss you. So he has to tell you how he feels in words."

Monday, December 7th. Still Homeroom

We have exams next week. I have English and Algebra on the same day.

On December 17th I have Biology. I'm not very good at Biology. I'm not flunking it because Kenny gives me the answers to the homework. But if I break up with Kenny, he won't let me copy his answers anymore.

On December 18th, in the evening, there is the Winter Dance. But Kenny hasn't asked me to the dance yet.

If I break up with Kenny, I won't be able to go to the dance. You can't go without a date. You can't go alone.

Monday, December 7th. Later

I talked to my friend, Tina Hakim Baba, beween lessons earlier today. I told her what Kenny said last night on the phone.

Tina is a good friend. Her father comes from Saudi Arabia and he owns an oil company. He is afraid that kidnappers may try and take Tina away. So Tina has a bodyguard, like me. Her bodyguard's name is Wahim.

Tina believed me about Kenny. She thought it was great.

"Oh, Mia, you are so lucky," she said.

"But, Tina," I said. "I don't love Kenny."

Tina opened her eyes wide.

"You don't?" she said.

"No," I said sadly. "I really like him, as a friend. But I'm not in love *with him*."

"Oh Mia," Tina said, grabbing[23] my arm. "There's someone else, isn't there?"

There were only a few minutes before the bell for our next class. But suddenly I decided to tell Tina everything.

"Yes," I replied.

"I knew it!" shouted Tina excitedly. "So who is he?"

"It doesn't matter," I said. "Besides[24], he has a girlfriend."

"It's Michael, isn't it?" said Tina.

At first, I wanted to say no. But perhaps Tina might be able to help me.

"If you tell anyone, I'll kill you,' I said. "Do you understand? I'LL KILL YOU."

Then Tina became very excited and started jumping up and down.

"I knew it," she said. "Oh, Mia, I've always thought you and Michael would make a lovely couple."

I was happy because Tina hadn't laughed at me. I wanted to throw my arms around her but there was no time. The bell for our next lesson was soon going to ring.

"Really?" I said. "You don't think it's stupid?"

"No," Tina said. Then she looked worried. "But what about Kenny? And Judith?"

"I know," I said sadly. "Tina, I don't know what to do."

Then the bell rang. We were both very late to class. But I didn't mind because now I don't have to worry alone any more. Tina is worrying with me.

Monday, December 7th. Later

A terrible thing happened in the school cafeteria at lunch. I met Michael and I asked him about his dentist appointment. Then Michael told me what the dentist had done. As he talked, I looked at his lips. Michael has very nice lips. They look like they would be very soft to kiss.

Michael has very nice lips. They look like they would be very soft to kiss.

And RIGHT THEN, Kenny went by to get his lunch.

I know Kenny can't read my mind. But he didn't say "hi" when Michael and I said "hi." He must have seen that my face was red. I mean, I was wondering what it would be like to kiss Michael's lips, when my boyfriend walked by.

I'm sure Michael's going out with Judith Gershner. After he got his lunch, he sat down next to her.

I wish I were leaving for Genovia tomorrow.

Monday, December 7th. French class

Lilly is mad with Mrs Spears, her English teacher. Lilly has to write a paper for English. She wanted to write about everything that's wrong with the Albert Einstein High School. But Mrs Spears didn't approve of [25] Lilly's ideas so she told Lilly to write about something else.

Now Lilly wants to arrange a protest [26] against the school. She wants all the students to walk out of their lessons tomorrow. This was our conversation.

LILLY: I think we should have a walkout.

ME: A walkout?

LILLY: You know. We all get up and walk out of school at the same time. We do it to show the teachers that we're not happy.

ME: Lilly, I don't think that this week's a good time for a walkout. It's almost our final exams. I can't miss any classes. I don't want my grades to get any worse.

At that moment the bell rang, so I don't think Lilly will have time to arrange a walkout. That's a good thing, because I really need the extra study time.

4

Grandmere's Advice

Monday, December 7th. Biology class
Kenny has just passed me the following note.

> Mia—I hope what I said to you last night didn't make
> you feel uncomfortable. I just wanted you to know how
> I felt.
>   Kenny

He's sitting here next to me, waiting for an answer. Maybe this is the perfect time to break up with him. I could simply write,

> I'm sorry, Kenny, but I don't feel the same way—let's just be friends.

But I don't want to upset Kenny. And he's my Biology partner. I mean, I'm going to have to sit by him for the next two weeks. And what about the Winter Dance? If I break up with Kenny, who will take me?

But what else can I do? After what happened at lunch today?

> Dear Kenny,
> I think of you as a very dear friend . . .

Monday, December 7th, 3:00 p.m. Mr Gianini's Algebra class
The bell rang before I could finish my note to Kenny.

I'm going to call him tonight and tell him how I feel.

Tuesday, December 8th. Homeroom

Well, I didn't break up with Kenny.

After my Algebra lesson with Mr Gianini, I went to the showroom where Sebastiano is selling his new designs. I had to be measured for my new dress.

Grandmere was there with her dog, Rommel. She was drinking her favorite cocktail.

Sebastiano started to talk about my dress. But I wasn't listening to him. I was busy thinking about my problems with Kenny.

Suddenly Grandmere put down her cocktail and shouted, "Amelia, what's the matter with you?"

"What?" I said.

Grandmere gave me an angry look.

"Sebastiano," my grandmother said. "Please leave the princess and myself alone for a moment."

Sebastiano left the room.

"Now," Grandmere said. "Something is worrying you, Amelia. What is it? Trouble at home? Your mother and the Algebra teacher are fighting already, I suppose?"

I felt very angry when Grandmere said that.

"My mom and Mr Gianini are very happy," I said. "I wasn't thinking about them at all."

"What is it, then?" asked Grandmere.

"Nothing," I almost shouted. "I just—well, I have to break up with my boyfriend tonight."

"Oh?" said Grandmere in an interested voice. "What boyfriend?"

"I have only one boyfriend," I said. "His name is Kenny."

"I thought this Kenny person was your Biology partner," said Grandmere.

"He is," I said. "He's also my boyfriend. But the other night, he told me that he loves me."

Grandmere patted Rommel on the head.

"And what is wrong," she asked, "about a boy who says that he loves you?"

"Nothing," I said. "But I'm not in love with him. So it's not right."

"Why not?" said Grandmere. "Unless, of course, you are in love with someone else. Is there someone special in your life, Amelia?"

"No," I lied.

"You're lying," said Grandmere. "You have a very bad habit, Amelia. When you lie, your nostrils[27] flare—they become much wider. If you do not believe me, look at your nose in the mirror."

I turned around to face the mirror. My nostrils weren't flaring. Grandmere was crazy.

"I'll ask you again," said Grandmere. "Are you in love with anyone?"

"No," I lied.

And my nostrils flared! Grandmere was right. All these years, no-one has ever told me about my nostrils flaring when

I lie—not even my mother or Lilly!

"Fine," I cried, turning around from the mirror. "All right, yes, *I am* in love with someone else."

"Don't shout, Amelia," said Grandmere. "Who is this special someone?"

"I'm not going to tell you," I said.

"Does he feel the same way about you?" asked Grandmere.

"No," I replied. "He likes another girl who knows how to clone fruit flies."

"How useful," said Grandmere. "Well, Amelia, do not throw away this Kenny until you have got someone better."

I stared at Grandmere. I felt very shocked. How could she say such cold things?

"What about the Winter Dance?" said Grandmere. "If you stop seeing Kenny, who will take you to the dance?"

"I won't go with anybody," I said. "I'll just stay home."

"While everyone else has a good time? And what about this other young man? The one you are in love with. Will he be at the dance with the house fly girl?"

"Fruit fly," I said. "And I don't know."

Would Michael ask Judith Gershner to the Winter Dance? When I thought about this I began to feel sick.

"One way to make this young man notice you," Grandmere went on, "is to go to the dance with the other young man. You should look very beautiful in a dress designed by Genovian fashion designer, Sebastiano Grimaldi."

"Grandmere," I said. "This boy likes smart girls. He isn't going to notice me just because I'm wearing a pretty dress."

"Hmmm," said Grandmere. "Do what you want. But it seems cruel, breaking up with Kenny at this time of year."

"Why?" I asked. "Because it's Christmas?"

"No," Grandmere said. "Because you both have your exams. But you must do what you think is best."

I felt terrible. Of course, I can't break up with Kenny now. You can't break up with someone just before Finals.

I *want* to break up with Kenny, but I can't.

I *want* to tell Michael how I feel about him, but I can't.

Tuesday, December 8th. English class

Something really embarrassing happened in the third-floor hallway between lessons. I talked about it with my friend, Shameeka.

SHAMEEKA: What happened in the hallway just now? Did Kenny just say what I think he said?

ME: Yes. Oh, Shameeka, what am I going to do?

SHAMEEKA: What do you mean? The boy loves you, Mia.

ME: Do you think everyone heard him? Do you think the people coming out of their Chemistry lesson heard him?

SHAMEEKA: Yes, of course. He shouted it very loudly.

ME: Were they laughing? The people coming out of Chemistry? They weren't laughing, were they?

SHAMEEKA: Most of them were laughing. Except Michael. He wasn't laughing.

ME: HE WASN'T? REALLY? Are you joking?

SHAMEEKA: No. Why would I be joking? And why do you care what Michael Moscovitz thinks?

ME: I don't care. People shouldn't go around laughing at other people's problems, that's all.

SHAMEEKA: I don't see the problem. So Kenny loves you. A lot of girls would like it if their boyfriend shouted "I love you" at them.

ME: Yeah, well, NOT ME!!!!!

5

My Plan

Tuesday, December 8th. Biology class

We have a class in school where we work on our own special projects. I usually enjoy this class because Michael helps me with my Algebra homework. But today it wasn't fun at all.

Judith Gershner came. She had her arm around the back of Michael's chair. Then she interrupted a private conversation I was having with Lilly about Kenny.

"I heard what Kenny said to you in the hallway," Judith said. "He said, 'I don't care if you don't feel the same way, Mia, I will always love you.' It's really sweet."

"He really knows how he feels," replied Lilly. "Not like Mia."

This made me mad. I know exactly how I feel. But I just can't tell anyone.

I was very surprised when Michael suddenly spoke.

"Mia doesn't shout about her feelings in the third-floor hallway," said Michael. "But she still knows how she feels."

"Yeah," I said in a pleased voice.

"Well, why didn't you tell Kenny that you love him too?" asked Lilly.

"Look," I answered, feeling my cheeks turn red. "I really like Kenny as a friend. But love, I mean *love*. That is a very big thing. I'm not, I mean, I don't . . ."

I stopped. Everyone in the room was listening, especially Michael.

"I see," said Lilly. "You're afraid to say that you love a guy for ever."

"I'm not afraid," I said. "There are many boys who . . ."

"Oh, yeah?" said Lilly. "So make a list. Make a list of boys who you could love for ever."

I made a list of ten boys. But Lilly said my list was no good. Except for one, the boys were all from films. The only *real* boy on my list was Justin Baxendale, a good-looking senior boy. Justin has just come to the Albert Einstein High School from Trinity, a school for rich boys.

Of course, I couldn't put Michael's name on my list. Michael was there, sitting next to his girlfriend, Judith Gershner.

Kenny just passed me a note.

Mia—I'm sorry that I embarrassed you today. Sometimes I forget that you are still quite shy. I promise never to do that again. I know you like Chinese food. Will you have lunch with me at Big Wong on Thursday?
Kenny.

Tuesday, December 8th, 7:00 p.m.
I had a princess lesson today. Grandmere kept asking me about Kenny. She said that Kenny was very clever to send me those anonymous love letters.

"What was so clever about those letters?" I asked.

"Well, you're his girlfriend now, aren't you?" Grandmere replied.

I hadn't thought about it before, but I think Grandmere's right.

Tuesday, December 8th, 8:30 p.m.
Lilly has sent an email to every kid in the school. She wrote,

To all students at Albert Einstein High School.
Do you feel worried and nervous because of too many exams? A silent walkout has been planned for tomorrow at 10 a.m. Leave your pencils, leave your books and

```
walk outside the school to East 75th Street. The
walkout is to protest against Principal Gupta and the
school. Show your teachers how you feel!
```

I don't know what to do. I can't just walk out of school tomorrow at 10 a.m. That's Mr Gianini's Algebra lesson. He will be upset if we get up and leave.

But if I don't take part in the walkout, Lilly will be mad.

Tuesday, December 8th, 8:45 p.m.

I just got this instant message on my computer from Michael. We often chat in an internet chatroom. Michael always uses the name "CracKing"—a criminal who sells drugs. I use "FtLouie" which means "Fat Louie"—the name of my cat.

```
CracKing: Did you just get that crazy e-mail from my
sister? You're not going to take part in her stupid
walkout, are you?
FtLouie: But she'll be mad with me if I don't.
CracKing: You don't have to do everything she says,
Mia. You don't always agree to do everything she wants.
FtLouie: But it's EASIER to do what she wants.
CracKing: Well, I'm not walking out.
FtLouie: It's different for you. You're her brother.
You live together.
CracKing: Not for much longer.
```

Michael has been accepted by Columbia College, one of the best colleges in New York. He's going there in the fall. So is Judith Gershner.

```
FtLouie: That's right. You got accepted by Columbia.
Congratulations. You must be happy because you'll know
one other person there—Judith Gershner.
```

CracKing: Yeah. Listen, are you still going to be in
town for the Winter Carnival²⁸? You're not leaving for
Genovia before the 18th, are you?

The Winter Carnival is after our finals on December
18th. All the school clubs will have special booths²⁹ at the
carnival. The Winter Dance is in the evening, after the
carnival. But Michael isn't going to ask me to the dance.
He must know I'm going with Kenny, that is if Kenny ever
asks me. Besides, isn't Michael going with Judith?

FtLouie: I'm leaving for Genovia on the 19th.
CracKing: Oh, good. Because you should come to the
Computer Club's booth at the carnival. I want you to
see this new program I've been working on.

Of course Michael isn't going to ask me to the dance. He
just wants me to look at his stupid computer program.
    I wanted to write,

Don't you know how I feel? Don't you know that the only
guy I could love for ever is YOU?

But instead I wrote:

FtLouie: I can't wait. Well, I have to go now. Bye.

Wednesday, December 9th, 3:00 a.m.
I've just woken up with these words going around in my head.
    "Well you're his girlfriend now, aren't you?"
    That's what Grandmere said about Kenny's love letters.
I THINK SHE'S RIGHT.
    Kenny's anonymous letters did work. I mean, I AM his
girlfriend now.

So why don't I write some anonymous love letters to the boy *I* like? I think that's a good plan.

Wednesday, December 9th. Homeroom

I told Tina about my plan this morning. Tina thought it was a great idea too. So before school started, we went to our local shop to buy a card.

I wanted a card that had no message inside, with a nice picture on the front. But the only blank cards had photos of fruit. The best one was of a strawberry.

Tina agreed to write a poem on the inside of the card. I didn't want to write it myself because I didn't want Michael to recognize my handwriting. I didn't want him to know the card was from me.

So Tina wrote,

> Roses are red
> Violets[30] are blue
> You may not know it
> But someone loves you.

I wasn't sure about using "the L word"—"*Love.*" I wanted to use "Like." But Tina said "Love" was right.

Because, as she said, "It's the truth, isn't it?"

Tina's going to put the card into Michael's locker[31].

6

The Walkout

Wednesday, December 9th, 9:30 a.m.
I just saw Lilly in the hallway. She whispered, "DON'T
FORGET! TEN O'CLOCK!"

Well, I *did* forget. The walkout! Her stupid walkout!

Mr Gianini is standing in front of the class. He doesn't
know about the walkout. It's not his fault Mrs Spears didn't
like Lilly's paper.

It's already nine thirty-five. What am I going to do?

Wednesday, December 9th, 9:45 a.m.
Lana Weinberger just said, "Are you going to walk out with
your fat friend?"

Lana is in my grade and she's beautiful. She's going out
with Josh Richter, a very good-looking boy. But Lana is
always saying mean things about me and my friends. I'm very
angry with Lana for saying Lilly's fat. Lilly isn't fat. She's
just round.

Wednesday, December 9th, 9:50 a.m.
Ten minutes until the walkout. I have to leave the classroom.

Wednesday, December 9th, 9:55 a.m.
I told Mr Gianini I had to go to the bathroom and he gave
me a hall pass. If a teacher asks why I am not in my class, I
can show them this pass.

I'm standing in the hallway next to the fire alarm[32]. Lars is
with me. And Justin Baxendale just walked by with a hall
pass too. He gave us a really weird look.

Justin Baxendale's eyelashes are really long and dark . . .

I CAN'T BELIEVE I AM WRITING ABOUT JUSTIN BAXENDALE'S EYELASHES AT A TIME LIKE THIS.

I have a big problem. If I don't walk out with Lilly, I'll lose my best friend.

But if I do walk out, I'll upset my stepfather.

There's only one thing I can do to stop the walkout.

I just told Lars to get ready to run.

Wednesday, December 9th, 10:00 a.m. On East 75th Street

We're all standing in the middle of 75th Street in the rain. Nobody has coats on. When they heard the fire alarm, the teachers made everyone run outside very quickly. There wasn't any time to get our coats.

Lilly is really mad, but I don't know why. She wanted everyone to leave the school and go outside. And that's what happened. Of course, Lilly wanted us to go outside to protest against the school, not because a fire alarm sounded.

'Somebody told the teachers about our walkout!" she shouted. "So they arranged a practice fire drill[33] at the same time!"

Wednesday, December 9th. Special Project class

I don't know if Michael got the card or not!!!!!

Stupid Judith Gershner is here in our class again. I suppose Michael must want her to be here. And because Michael is so busy with Judith, I suppose I'll have to do Algebra by myself.

That's all right. I can study very well on my own. Who needs Michael's help? Not me.

Wednesday, December 9th. French class

I'm worried because I know very little about kissing. So I think I should get some advice from a kissing expert like

Tina Hakim Baba. Tina knows a lot about kissing. She has been kissing her boyfriend, Dave Farouq El-Abar, for almost three months now.

So I wrote down some questions for Tina and she answered them for me.

Tina—I need to know about kissing. Can you please answer each of the following questions?????? Mia

1. Does a boy know if a girl doesn't know how to kiss?
The boy may know you are nervous. But everyone is nervous when they kiss someone new. It's weird kissing someone for the first time. But it's fun too.

2. How do you know when it's time to stop?
Stop when you feel like you've had enough.

3. If you're in love with him, is it still horrible?
Of course not! Kissing is never horrible! But it's always better kissing someone you really like.

4. If he's in love with you, does he care if you are a bad kisser?
If the guy likes/loves you, he won't care if you are a good kisser or not.

Wednesday, December 9th, 9:00 p.m. In the limousine[34] coming home from Grandmere's suite

I am so tired. Grandmere took me to Sebastiano's showroom and made me try on every dress there. There were short dresses, long dresses, and dresses with straight skirts. There were dresses with wide skirts, white ones, pink ones, blue ones, and even a bright green dress.

I have to choose a dress to wear on Genovian national TV on Christmas Eve. But Sebastiano is a very good designer.

*Grandmere took me to Sebastiano's showroom
and made me try on every dress there.*

There were several dresses I really liked.

I told Sebastiano about the Winter Dance. Then Sebastiano started asking me questions like,

"Who do you go with?" and "What he look like?"

Suddenly, I started telling Sebastiano all about my love life. I told him about Kenny, and how Kenny loves me but I don't love him. I told him how I love someone else, but he doesn't love me.

Sebastiano is a very good listener. When I had finished, he said,

"This boy you like. How you know he no like you back?"

"Because," I explained, "he likes this other girl."

Sebastiano waved his hands.

"No, no, no. He help you with your Al home. (Sebastiano only says the first syllable of English words. He meant "Algebra homework".) Why he do that if he no like you?"

"Because I'm his little sister's best friend." I said sadly.

"You no worry," said Sebastiano. "I make dress. After dance, this boy no think of you as little sister's best friend."

One of Sebastiano's assistants took photos of me in all the dresses. Sebastiano wants me to see how I look in each one. Then I can decide which dress I like best.

Today, Mr Gianini asked me some questions after class.

MR GIANINI: Mia, I heard a story about a walkout. People were saying that the students were planning to walk out of classes this morning. Had you heard about that?

ME: (*very nervously*): Um, no.

MR GIANINI: So you wouldn't know if someone, to stop the protest, turned on the fire alarm on the second floor?

ME: Um, no.

MR GIANINI: Do you know the punishment for turning on a fire alarm when there is no fire? Anyone who did that would have to leave the school.

ME: Oh, yes. I know that.

MR GIANINI: I gave you a hall pass shortly before the alarm went off. So I thought maybe you were in the hall and saw the person who did it.

ME: Oh, no. I didn't see anybody.

MR GIANINI: I didn't think so. Oh, well. If you ever hear who did it, maybe you could tell *her* from me never to do it again.

ME: Um, OK.

MR GIANINI: And tell *her* "thanks" from me too. It's a difficult time right now, with all the worry about Finals. (*Mr Gianini picked up his briefcase and jacket*). See you at home.

Then Mr Gianini smiled at me. But he couldn't know that I was the person who turned on the fire alarm. I knew my nostrils were flaring. But Mr Gianini doesn't know that my nostrils flare when I lie. RIGHT????

Thursday, December 10th. Homeroom

Lilly keeps talking about everything that is wrong with the Albert Einstein High School. She is organizing a meeting of a new protest group on Saturday morning. She says that I have to be the group's secretary because I'm good at writing things down.

Michael has gone to school early every day this week. He's working on his computer program for the Winter Carnival.

I bought another card last night from the gift shop at the Plaza Hotel. This card is better than that stupid one with the strawberry. It has a picture of a lady holding a finger to her lips. Inside, it says, *Shhh . . . . .*

Under that, I'm going to ask Tina to write:

Roses are red
But cherries are redder
Maybe she can clone fruit flies
But I like you better.

7
Another Crime

Thursday, December 10th, 11:00.am.

Principal Gupta called a meeting of the whole school this morning. She asked if anyone had any information about Wednesday's fire alarm.

I'm not worried. The only person who could give her information about me is Justin Baxendale. He passed me in the hallway a few minutes before I turned on the alarm. But Justin Baxendale isn't listening to Principal Gupta. He's playing games on his Gameboy.

Thursday, December 10th. Special Project class

Today was my lunch with Kenny at Big Wong.

Kenny still hasn't asked me to the Winter Dance. And I don't think he loves me as much as he says. He's stopped calling me after school. He says it's because he's busy studying for Finals, but I suspect[35] something else.

I think Kenny knows how I feel about Michael.

I'm not enjoying our Special Project class today. Judith Gershner isn't here . . . but neither is Michael. Nobody knows where he is.

Thursday, December 10th, 9:00 p.m.

Tonight, when I went for my princess lesson with Grandmere, Sebastiano was there too.

When Grandmere paused to take a phone call, Sebastiano started asking me lots of questions. He wanted to know what clothes my friends and I like to wear. He wrote my answers down in a little notebook.

When Grandmere finished her phone call, I told her that I couldn't come to princess lessons next week. I explained that I had SIX Finals to prepare for. But Grandmere was not very pleased.

Fortunately, my dad came in just then. I told him about my Finals and that I didn't have time to go to my princess lessons.

"Yes, of course," he said. Grandmere started to argue, but my dad said,

"If Mia hasn't learnt how to be a princess by this time, she never will."

Grandmere pressed her lips together and didn't say anything more.

Friday, December 11th. Homeroom

Here's what I have to do:
1. Stop thinking about Michael when I should be studying.
2. Stop telling Grandmere anything about my personal life.
3. Start acting more
   A. Grown up.
   B. Like a princess.
4. Stop biting my fingernails.
5. Write down everything Mom and Mr Gianini need to know about taking care of Fat Louie when I'm away in Genovia.
6. BUY CHRISTMAS PRESENTS!
7. Stop watching TV when I should be studying.
8. Stop playing computer games when I should be studying.
9. Stop listening to music when I should be studying.
10. Break up with Kenny.

Friday, December 11th. Principal Gupta's Office
I've done a terrible thing.

I, Mia Thermopolis, have become a young criminal. The fire alarm was only the beginning. Maybe I'll even have to leave the school. But it's not my fault. It's Lana's fault.

I was sitting in Mr Gianini's Algebra lesson. Lana was sitting at the desk in front of me. Then she turned around and put a newspaper, *USA Today*, on my desk. There was an article with a big headline:

Most Popular Young Royal

Fifty-seven per cent of our readers have voted for *Prince William* of England as their favorite young royal, while Will's little brother *Harry* has twenty-eight per cent. *Princess Mia Renaldo* of Genovia is in third place, with thirteen per cent of the votes. Why is Princess Mia so unpopular?

I read the stupid article and gave the paper back to Lana. "So?" I whispered to her.

"So," Lana whispered. "I wonder how popular you would be if their readers knew that you turned on fire alarms."

I was very shocked. How did Lana know I had turned on the fire alarm? She couldn't have seen me. Unless . . .

Unless Justin Baxendale had told her.

I don't know why I behaved like I did, but something happened inside me. Lana's little pink cell phone was lying on top of her desk. Suddenly, I reached for it and put it on the floor. I crushed[36] it with my boot and it broke into hundreds of pieces.

So Mr Gianini sent me to the principal's office. I can't really blame him, even if he is my stepfather.

Oh. Here comes Principal Gupta.

Friday, December 11th, 5:00 p.m. The Loft[37]

I've been suspended[38] from school so I have to stay at home. It's only for one day. But they're going to write it on my school record. They're treating me like a criminal.

I'm not a criminal. My dad doesn't think so, either. But I'm not going to tell my dad why I broke Lana's cell phone. I'm not going to tell him about the fire alarm.

Now I'm at home with my mother. I'm sitting on her bed and we're watching TV. Because Mom is pregnant she is often tired, so she spends a lot of time in bed.

Mom was drawing some pictures of me. Then she asked me questions about what Lana had said. She wanted to know why I had crushed Lana's cell phone. Suddenly I started telling her a lot of things. I told her all about Kenny, and Michael, and Judith Gershner, and Tina and the anonymous cards, and the Winter Carnival, and Lilly and her walkout. I told her everything, except about the fire alarm.

After a while, my mom stopped drawing.

"You know what I think you need?" she said. "A vacation."

So then we had a sort of vacation, right there on her bed. I ordered pizzas, and then we watched some great movies. For a while, it was almost like the old days. You know, before my mom met Mr Gianini and I found out I was a princess.

44

Friday, December 11th, 8:00 p.m. The Loft

I just checked my email. I have a lot of messages from my friends. They all think I did a very good thing when I crushed Lana's cell phone.

But I only did it to hide my other crime. I was afraid Lana would tell everyone that I had turned on the fire alarm.

Something good: Michael is getting my cards. Tina walked by his locker today and saw him put the latest card into his bag!

I've just got an Instant Message from Michael on my computer!

CracKing: Hey, Thermopolis, what's this I hear about you getting suspended?

I wrote back:

FtLouie: Just for one day.
CracKing: What did you do?
FtLouie: I crushed Lana Weinberger's cell phone.
CracKing: Are your parents making you stay at home?
FtLouie: No. I told them I attacked Lana's phone because of something she said.
CracKing: So you're still going to the Carnival?
FtLouie: Yes.

This is the second time Michael's asked me if I'm going to the Winter Carnival.

Friday, December 11th, 9:00 p.m.

Mr Gianini got home late tonight. He stopped on his way home to buy a huge Christmas tree.

I don't approve of people cutting down trees for Christmas. But I didn't say anything about the tree because my mom was so excited. Mr Gianini kept looking at me, to see if I was happy too. He said that he had got the tree because I'd had a bad day. He wanted to do something nice for me.

8

Sebastiano in Trouble

Saturday, December 12th, 2:00 p.m. Lilly's apartment
The meeting of Lilly's new protest group took place[39] today.
But nobody came except me and Lilly's boyfriend, Boris
Pelkowski.

Lilly's very upset that only Boris and I came to her
meeting. I try to tell her that everyone is too busy studying
for Finals. Boris is sitting beside her and speaking to her in a
calm voice. Boris wears weird clothes, but you can see he
really loves Lilly.

It makes my heart hurt, when I see Boris looking at Lilly
like that. I must be jealous. I want a boy to look *at me* like
that. But I don't mean Kenny.

I can't watch Lilly and Boris anymore. I'm going into the
kitchen to see what Maya, the Moscovitzs' housekeeper, is
doing. Maybe I can help her.

Saturday, December 12th, 2:30 p.m. Lilly's apartment
Maya wasn't in the kitchen. She's here, in Michael's room,
putting away Michael's school uniform.

It's very interesting to be in Michael's room. I have been
in it before, but only when Michael was here. But now he's at
school, working on the computer project for the Winter
Carnival.

I am lying on Michael's bed, while Maya puts his shirts
away. I'm looking up at his ceiling and over at his desk.

I've just noticed something. My card with the picture of
the strawberry is right there on his desk.

I feel happy that Michael hasn't thrown away my cards!

Oh. I just heard the front door open. Is it Michael??? Or
his parents??? I had better get out of his room.

46

Saturday, December 12th, 3:00 p.m. Grandmere's suite, the Plaza Hotel

Sebastiano is in big trouble.

When I visited Sebastiano's showroom, he made me try on all the new dresses he had designed. Then one of his assistants took photos of me.

Sebastiano's sold the photos to the *Sunday Times* magazine! When Lilly's parents—the Drs Moscovitz—came in, they had a copy of the magazine.

"So you're a model[40] now, Mia!" they said to me. "Congratulations!"

"What are you talking about?" I asked in surprise.

Then the Drs Moscovitz showed me an article with the heading *Fashion for a Princess*. Underneath, there were about twenty photos of me wearing Sebastiano's new dresses.

It's a great way for Sebastiano to advertize his dresses. When women see pictures of a princess wearing his dresses, they'll want to buy them.

I was trying on these dresses because I wanted something nice to wear on Genovian national TV. But when people see those pictures, they'll think I'm only interested in clothes.

My father is really mad with Sebastiano. He thinks Sebastiano has used me to sell his clothes. I'm upset too. But Grandmere can't understand why my dad and I are so mad.

"You look really beautiful," she keeps saying.

My dad has called the concierge[41] of the Plaza Hotel. Dad told him not to let Sebastiano back into the hotel.

Saturday, December 12th, 5:00 p.m. The Loft

It's not Sebastiano's fault about the pictures. It's Grandmere's. I don't think my dad will ever speak to her again. I know Grandmere is an old lady, but she didn't think about my feelings at all.

Sebastiano called when I was getting ready to leave. He was very surprised that my dad is so mad. He said that he had tried to come upstairs to see us, but the concierge stopped him.

When my dad told Sebastiano he was very upset about the photos, Sebastiano was even more surprised.

"But I had your permish, Philippe!" he kept saying. (Sebastiano meant "permission.")

"You did not!" said my dad.

Then Sebastiano said that he had got permission from Grandmere.

"I only did it, Philippe," said Grandmere, "because Amelia is so shy. I wanted her to feel better about herself."

But my dad wouldn't listen to her. He came over, grabbed

my arm and took me out of the hotel suite. Then he asked Lars to take me home.

When I get to school on Monday, everyone is going to say, "Oh, look, here's Mia. She says she's only interested in animal rights and being a vegetarian. But now she's become a fashion model!"

Saturday, December 12th, 8:00 p.m. The Loft

I already have seventeen emails, six phone calls and one visit (Lilly) from people who saw the pictures.

Why are all these people calling and e-mailing me? How do I explain that I didn't *know* about the pictures? Nobody is going to believe me.

Millions of people will see the pictures and think, "How much did the newspaper pay Princess Mia for those pictures?"

Now I have to start studying. I'm going to study Algebra first because it's my worst subject. It's also my first test.

I WILL PASS ALGEBRA THIS SEMESTER!!!!!!

Saturday, December 12th, 9:00 p.m. The Loft

Mom and Mr Gianini are watching a really good movie in the next room. So I went and watched my favorite part of the movie with them. But now I'm studying again.

Saturday, December 12th, 9:30 p.m. The Loft

Four of the seventeen emails were from Michael. One was about my pictures in the magazine and the other three were jokes. They weren't very funny, but I laughed anyway.

I'm sure Judith Gershner doesn't laugh at Michael's jokes. She's too busy cloning fruit flies.

Saturday, December 12th, 10:00 p.m. The Loft

I've just written out some instructions for my mom and Mr

Gianini about Fat Louie. I've told them how to take care of him while I'm away in Genovia.

Saturday, December 12th, Midnight. The Loft
I can't believe it's midnight already and I am still only on Chapter One of *An Introduction to Algebra!*

Sunday, December 13th, 10:30 a.m. The Loft
Lilly just came over. She wants us to study for our exams together.

Sunday, December 13th, Noon. The Loft
Michael told Boris where Lilly was, so now Boris is here too.

Boris breathes very loudly so I can't pay attention to my studies. And I wish he wouldn't put his feet on my bed. I wanted him to take his shoes off first. But Lilly said Boris's feet smell.

How can Lilly be happy with a boyfriend who breathes loudly and whose feet smell?

Sunday, December 13th, 12:30 p.m. The Loft
Now Kenny's here.

Sunday, December 13th, 8:00 p.m. The Loft
After Boris and Kenny arrived, it was impossible to do any more studying. So we decided to go to Chinatown, the Chinese area of New York. We went to a restaurant called Great Shanghai and had a really good time.

Now I'm home again. My mom says that while I was out, Sebastiano called four times. AND he sent a dress to my home.

He designed this dress for me to wear to the Winter Dance. It's made of dark green velvet with long sleeves. It isn't sexy. But when I put it on and looked at myself in the mirror, I looked really good.

There was a note attached to the dress that said:

Please forgive[42] me.
I promise this dress will not make him think of you as his little sister's best friend.

Of course I forgive Sebastiano. And I expect one day I'll forgive Grandmere too. But I will never forgive myself. I should just have told Sebastiano, "No photos."

But when I was looking at myself in all those beautiful dresses, I forgot that being a princess is not just about wearing pretty dresses. Being a princess is about behaving as a good example to a lot of people . . . even people you don't know, and may never meet.

9

Yellow Roses

Monday, December 14th. Homeroom

When I got to my locker this morning, I was very surprised. A yellow rose was sticking out of the door. What can this mean? But when I looked around, I saw only Justin Baxendale with a crowd of girls.

I suppose the person who is leaving me anonymous roses must be Kenny.

It's Reading Day today. We are supposed to spend the day studying in homeroom. Our Finals begin tomorrow.

Kenny keeps passing me little notes. They say things like: *Keep smiling!*

It's five days until the Winter Dance, and I still don't have a date.

Tuesday, December 15th

The Algebra and English Finals are finished. I have only three more exams.

Someone left another yellow rose in my locker. I asked Kenny if it was him, but he said no. Then Justin Baxendale walked by.

Four more days until the Winter Dance, and *still* no date.

Wednesday, December 16th

I have only two more exams left.

There was another yellow rose today.

Three more days until the dance. Still nothing.

Thursday, December 17th, 1:00 a.m.
Maybe Kenny is lying about the roses. Maybe they really are from him. Maybe he's leaving them for me as a kind of joke, before he asks me to the dance tomorrow night.

Thursday, December 17th, 4:00 p.m. In the limousine on the way to the Plaza Hotel
MY FINALS ARE FINISHED!!!!!

I think I passed all of them. Even Algebra!

Now I can think about more important things. Everyone at school knows about those stupid photos in the magazine. So I am going to arrange a press conference[43]. I am going to call a meeting of TV reporters. I am going to tell them that Sebastiano is giving away *all* the money that he makes from the photos. He will give the money to Greenpeace[44].

Of course, Sebastiano doesn't know about this. And he isn't going to like it because he isn't going to make any money from advertizing those dresses. But then, he should have asked *me* if he could use my pictures to advertize his clothes.

I am very nervous. I've never arranged a press conference before. But I have to do it. The best part is, I'm doing it alone with no help from anyone.

Well, the concierge at the Plaza helped. He got me a room. And Lars made all the calls on his cell phone. And Lilly helped me write down what I was going to say, and Tina did my make-up and my hair.

But except for that, I did everything.

Thursday, December 17th, 7:00 p.m.
My press conference was very successful. I'm usually shy, but I think I spoke very well. I have now watched myself on the four major American TV networks.

My press conference was very successful.

Sebastiano called me right after the press conference. He was very angry. He kept shouting about how much money he had lost.

"Sebastiano," I said. "Everyone thinks you've done a wonderful thing. You've given all the money from the pictures to Greenpeace. So in the future, many more people will want to buy your clothes."

In the end, Sebastiano realized I was right. He stopped being angry and started to be happy.

Then my dad rang. He was laughing.

"You really know how to be a princess now," he said.

Thursday, December 17th, 9:00 p.m.

Tina just called. She didn't want to talk about the press conference. She asked what I got from my Secret Snowflake[45].

"Secret Snowflake?" I said in surprise. "What are you talking about?"

"You remember, Mia," said Tina. "Your Secret Snowflake. It's a kind of game. Some kids at school were organizing it about a month ago. We all wrote our names on pieces of paper. Then we put them in a jar. Then we all picked a piece of paper out of the jar. The person who picked your name is your Secret Snowflake. They have to buy you gifts in the last week of school. But you don't know who is giving you presents. You don't know who your Secret Snowflake is."

"Oh!" I cried. I had forgotten all about my Secret Snowflake. And I had forgotten that I had pulled Tina's name out of the jar. I had forgotten to buy any presents for her.

Then I realized something. The yellow roses. They must be from my Secret Snowflake!

"Have you bought gifts for your Secret Snowflake, Mia?" asked Tina.

"Uh, sure," I said. I felt terrible. Where was I was going to find a present for Tina? Tomorrow was the last day of the Secret Snowflake game.

"Finals are over now," Tina went on. "So when are you going to tell Michael that you sent him those cards?"

"I'm never going to tell him," I said.

"But Mia," said Tina, "then why did you send him the cards?"

"I wanted him to know that there are other girls who like him besides Judith Gershner," I replied.

"Mia," said Tina. "You have to tell him. How will you become his girlfriend if he doesn't know how you feel? That's how you became Kenny's girlfriend. He sent you the anonymous love letters, but then he told you he'd sent them.

"So you have to tell Michael it was you," Tina went on. "And you will have to tell him tomorrow. Because the next day you're leaving for Genovia."

I'd forgotten about that too. I am leaving for Genovia the day after tomorrow! With Grandmere! And I'm not even speaking to Grandmere anymore!

I told Tina that I'd tell Michael about the cards. She hung up the phone happily.

But I was lying to her.

I am never going to tell Michael how I feel about him.

I *can't*. Not ever.

Friday, December 18th. Homeroom
The teachers have just given us computer printouts[46] with our final exam grades. We can spend the rest of the day having fun at the Winter Carnival. And later this evening, at the dance.

I think I know who my Secret Snowflake is. It must be Justin Baxendale. I've seen him waiting near my locker three times this week. He must be leaving the roses for me.

We have to tell our Secret Snowflakes our names today. If Justin Baxendale tells me that he was my Secret Snowflake, I'm going to feel really embarrassed.

But I have worse problems than Justin Baxendale. I'm the only girl in the school who doesn't have a date for the dance tonight. And tomorrow, I have to leave for Genovia. I'm going there with my crazy grandmother who isn't speaking to my father.

I got a present for Tina. I went on the Internet and found a book club with romantic stories. I paid for her to become a member of the club. Now she can read new stories every month.

I'll have to go out to my locker when the bell rings. Perhaps Justin Baxendale will be there.

Tina says yellow roses mean 'love for ever'. That's why I thought they were from Kenny.

I have the computer printout with my exam grades. But I am not looking at it. I DO NOT CARE ABOUT MY GRADES.

The bell has just rung. I left the homeroom and now I'm standing by my locker. Justin is there, looking for someone. Lana is there too, waiting for her boyfriend, Josh.

"Dude[47]," Justin says.

Dude? I am not a dude. Who is Justin talking to?

I turn around. Josh is standing there, behind Lana.

"I've been looking for you all week," Justin is saying to Josh. "Do you have those Algebra notes for me?"

So Justin wasn't waiting for me, he was waiting for Josh!

Josh says something to Justin, but I don't hear him. Because Michael is standing behind Justin.

Michael Moscovitz.

And in his hand is *a yellow rose.*

57

10

A Big Shock

Friday, December 18th. At the Winter Carnival

When I saw Michael holding the yellow rose, I thought, "It's Michael! He has been leaving the yellow roses for me."

But then Michael said,

"Here. This just fell out of your locker."

I took the rose. My heart was beating very hard. But then I saw a note attached to the roses.

Good luck with your trip to Genovia!
See you when you get back!
Your Secret Snowflake,
Boris Pelkowski.

Boris Pelkowski has been sending me the yellow roses! Boris is my Secret Snowflake. Boris wouldn't know that yellow roses mean "love for ever".

"What grade did you get in Algebra?" said Michael.

I stared at him. I was still thinking about the roses. Then I opened the computer printout with my grades. To my surprise, I had got "B" for my Algebra grade. My last grade for an Algebra exam was "F". But I've worked hard at Algebra all semester and now my grade is a "B".

I was so happy that I forgot I was in love with Michael. I threw my arms around his neck.

Then Kenny came around the corner and saw me with my arms round Michael.

Now Tina says that Kenny thinks there's something going on between Michael and me. So I have to go and find Kenny. I have to tell him that Michael and I are just friends.

"Why don't you just tell Kenny the truth?" says Tina.

But you can't break up with someone during the Winter Carnival. That would be a really mean thing to do.

Friday, December 18th. Still at the Winter Carnival

Well, I couldn't find Kenny anywhere.

Tina's taking me over to the Computer Club's booth now. Michael and Judith and the rest of the kids in the Computer Club are sitting there behind their computers. They've designed a new computer game.

I don't want to go over to the Computer Club's booth. But Tina says I have to.

"It's the perfect time to tell Michael you love him," she says. "You have to tell him now, when Kenny isn't here."

Even Later on Friday, December 18th. Still at the Winter Carnival

Well, I'm in the Girls' Room again. And this time I'm never coming out.

When Tina and I arrived at the Computer Club's booth, Michael asked me to sit down in front of one of the computers. Then he told me to turn it on. So I sat there, waiting for the stupid computer game to start.

I was feeling very sad. No one had asked me to the dance. And tomorrow I'm going on a boring trip to Genovia. And before I go, I have to break up with Kenny. Then I'll leave for

Europe with my dad and Grandmere, who aren't speaking to each other. And when I come back, Michael and Judith will be engaged.

So I really didn't feel like playing a computer game.

But when the game started, I was surprised to see a picture of a castle with a garden. Inside the garden were red roses. It was very pretty.

Then a flag appeared on the computer screen. Some words were written on the flag in gold.

I screamed and jumped up. My chair fell over and everyone started laughing. Only Michael wasn't laughing.

But I couldn't look at Michael. What did it mean? Did

Michael feel the same way as I did? Or was it a kind of joke?

I knew I was going to start crying right there, in front of everyone. So I grabbed Tina's arm and pulled her towards the Girls' Room. I heard Michael shout, "Mia!" But I didn't stop. I pushed through the crowd, pulling Tina behind me.

Suddenly somebody grabbed my arm. It was Kenny.

"Mia, I have to talk to you," he said.

"Not *now*, Kenny," Tina said.

"Yes, *now*," Kenny said in a serious voice.

Tina let go of my arm and I stood there, waiting.

"Mia," said Kenny. "I just want to . . . I mean, I just want you to know. Well. That I know."

I stared at him. I had no idea what he was talking about.

"Look, Kenny," I said. "This really isn't a good time. Maybe we could talk later—'

"Mia," said Kenny. He had a funny look on his face. "I know. I saw him."

And then I remembered. Kenny had seen me with my arms round Michael after I got my "B" grade for Algebra.

"You don't have to worry," Kenny said. "I won't tell Lilly."

Lilly! I didn't want Lilly to know how I felt about Michael!

"Kenny," I said. "I am so, so sorry." Suddenly I started crying. When I put my hands to my face, they were wet with tears. "I really do like you," I went on. "I just don't . . . love you."

Kenny's face was white, but he didn't cry—not like me. He was smiling a weird little smile.

"I can't believe it," he said, shaking his head. "When I first realized what was happening, I thought, Mia would never do that to her best friend. But . . . well, I've suspected for a long time there was someone else. That's why you never wanted to kiss me.

"I knew you didn't want to hurt my feelings," Kenny went

on. "I didn't ask you to the dance because I knew you'd say no. Because you like someone else. I mean, I know you'd never lie to me, Mia. You're the most honest person I've ever met."

Was Kenny joking? Me? Honest?

"But I think you'd better tell Lilly soon," said Kenny. "I first suspected it at the restaurant. And if I suspected it, so will other people. You don't want someone else to tell her."

"Restaurant? What restaurant?" I asked in surprise.

"You know," replied Kenny. "That day we all went to Chinatown. You and he sat next to each other. You kept laughing . . . you were very friendly with each other."

"Chinatown?" I thought. But Michael hadn't gone with us that day to Chinatown. . .

"And I've noticed him leaving you yellow roses all week," said Kenny.

I stared at him through my tears.

"What?" I said.

"You know." He looked around, then whispered. "*Boris*. Leaving you all those roses."

BORIS. BORIS PELKOWSKI. I couldn't believe it. My boyfriend just broke up with me because he thinks I am in love with BORIS PELKOWSKI.

BORIS PELKOWSKI, who wears weird clothes.

BORIS PELKOWSKI, my best friend's boyfriend.

I tried to tell Kenny the truth. You know, that Boris isn't my secret love, but my Secret Snowflake.

But then Tina rushed forward.

"Sorry, Kenny," she said. "But Mia has to go now." Then she pulled me into the Girls' Room.

"I have to tell Kenny the truth," I kept saying.

"No, you don't," said Tina. "You two have broken up. All that matters is that you and Kenny are finished."

I looked at my face in the mirror. There were tears running down it.

Tina says that she's sure Michael didn't mean to make fun[48] of me. She says that he wanted to tell me he felt the same way about me.

If Michael was joking, it was a very cruel joke. Michael doesn't know how much I love him. He probably didn't mean to be cruel. He probably just thought that he was being funny.

I can't leave this bathroom. I'll just wait until everyone has gone, then I'll come out quietly and go home.

I'm going to Genovia tomorrow, and I'm going to stay there.

11

After the Winter Carnival

Friday, December 18th, 5:00 p.m. The Loft
I'm at home in my room. I've locked the door. I have to
pack for my trip to Genovia tomorrow. But people keep
calling and knocking on my door.

Well, I'm not talking to anybody. I'm not speaking to
Lilly, or my dad, or Mr Gianini or my mother, and
ESPECIALLY not Michael, although he's called me four
times.

**Friday, December 18th, 5:30 p.m. Outside on the Fire
Escape[49]**
I'm sitting on the fire escape outside my room. My dad told
Lars to remove my bedroom door so that people could get
into my bedroom. But I climbed out on to the fire escape
through my window.

It's snowing and it's very cold. But it's also really peaceful.
I can hear the soft sound of the snow all around me.

I hear footsteps from my room. Who's coming?

Friday, December 18th, 7:30 p.m.
Grandmere just climbed out of my bedroom window and
onto the fire escape to talk to me!

"Amelia," she said. "What are you doing out here? It's
snowing. Come inside."

I was really shocked that Grandmere spoke to me, after
what she did. She gave Sebastiano permission to take
pictures of me.

Then he used the pictures to advertize his clothes in the
newspapers.

"I understand that you are upset because of the pictures," said Grandmere. "But I wanted to show you that you are just as pretty as the other girls in those magazines."

Poor Grandmere. She comes from such a different world. In Grandmere's world, the most important thing for a girl is to be beautiful.

"I only meant to show you what you can do," said Grandmere. "And look what you did. You arranged a press conference all by yourself, and you passed Algebra."

I smiled. "That's true," I said.

"Now," Grandmere said, "there's only one thing left to do."

I nodded. "I know. It's best for me to live in Genovia."

Grandmere looked at me as if I were mad.

"Live in *Genovia?*" she said. "What are you talking about?"

"Maybe I could just finish school there," I said.

Grandmere just stared at me.

"But your friends . . . your mother . . ."

"Well," I said calmly. "They could come and visit."

Grandmere's face became hard.

'Amelia Mignonette Grimaldi Renaldo," she said. "You're running away from something, aren't you?" She got up from the fire escape and pointed at my window. "You get inside, right now," she said.

I was so surprised that I climbed back into my room through the window. Grandmere climbed in too. Then she went to my wardrobe and started looking through my clothes.

"You," she said, "are a princess of the royal family of Renaldo. And a princess does not run away when things go wrong."

She pulled out the green velvet dress which Sebastiano had designed for me. Then she stood there, waiting. I knew she wanted me to put on the dress.

"Grandmere," I said. "You don't understand. I can't go

"You are a princess of the royal family of Renaldo. And a princess does not run away when things go wrong."

back to the dance. I don't even have a date. And the whole school thinks I am in love with Boris Pelkowski."

"So you must show them that it doesn't matter what they think," said Grandmere. "Now get dressed, Mia."

I don't know why I obeyed her. Maybe it was because, deep inside me, I knew Grandmere was right.

But perhaps it was because, for the first time in my life, Grandmere didn't call me Amelia.

No. She called me Mia.

So I am sitting in the car right now. I'm going back to stupid Albert Einstein High School and wearing a stupid dress that Sebastiano designed.

We're here.

I think I'm going to be sick.

Saturday, December 18th. On the Royal Genovian Plane
Last night was the best night of my life. I have never been so happy. Not even on my sixth birthday when my mom gave me Fat Louie.

I am really grateful to Grandmere for making me go to that dance. I am SO GLAD I went back to Albert Einstein, the best, the greatest school in America.

When I walked into the school, Lilly-and-Boris and Tina-and-Dave came up. They seemed very happy to see me.

I went into the main hall. It was decorated like winter, with snowflakes everywhere. I saw Lana and her boyfriend, Josh. Justin Baxendale was with a group of girls. My friend Shameeka was there. Even Kenny was there.

Then I saw Judith Gershner in a red dress. She was dancing with a boy I had never seen before.

I went back to look for Lilly and found her making a telephone call.

"Where's your brother?" I asked.

"How should I know?" said Lilly.

"Well, Judith Gershner is here," I said, "so I thought . . ."

"How many times do I have to tell you?" said Lilly. *"Michael and Judith are not going out."*

"So why have they been spending time together?" I asked.

"Because they were working on that stupid computer program for the carnival," said Lilly. "Judith already has a boyfriend."

She grabbed my shoulders and turned me around so I could see Judith on the dance floor.

"He goes to Trinity," Lilly said.

I watched Judith dancing. The boy she was with looked like Kenny, but older.

"Oh," I said.

"You're behaving in a very weird way today," said Lilly. "Sit down here." She pulled out a chair. "And don't get up."

I sat down. Suddenly I felt very tired.

After a time, Lars and Wahim, Tina's bodyguard, came and sat next to me. I felt embarrassed, sitting with two bodyguards.

Nobody was asking me to dance. I had done what Grandmere wanted. I had come to the dance. But now I wanted to leave.

"Let's go," I said to Lars. "I have a lot of packing to do."

Lars started to get up. Then he stopped. I saw that he was looking at something behind me. I turned around.

And there was Michael. He had just arrived. There was fresh snow in his hair.

"I didn't think you were coming," he said. "I called you, but you wouldn't come to the phone. Mia, about what you saw on the computer today. I didn't mean to make you cry. Look, I knew it was you who was leaving those cards."

"You did?" I said.

I could feel my eyes filling with tears again.

68

"Of course I did," said Michael. "Lilly told me."

"*Lilly* told you?" I cried. "How did *she* know?"

He waved his hand impatiently.

"I don't know," he said. "Maybe your friend Tina told her. But that's not important."

I saw Lilly and Tina at the other end of the room. They were both staring at me. When they saw me looking at them, they turned away quickly.

"I'm going to kill them," I said.

Michael reached out and grabbed my shoulders.

"Mia," he said. "It doesn't *matter*. What matters is that I meant what I wrote. And I thought you did too."

"Of course *I* meant it," I said.

Michael shook his head.

"Then why did you behave in that weird way at the carnival today?" he asked.

"Well, because . . . I thought you were laughing at me."

"Never," he said.

And suddenly Michael leaned down and kissed me, right on the lips. And I found out then that Tina was right.

If you're in love, kissing is the nicest thing in the world.

Michael told me he has been in love with me for a long time too. He's kept it a secret for almost as long as I have.

We had the most wonderful evening. We danced all night, until Lilly finally came up and said,

"Come on, it's snowing really hard. We have to leave."

Then Lars drove me home and Michael and I kissed good night outside my apartment, with the snow falling all around us.

That was last night. Now I'm on the plane to Genovia, with my dad sitting beside me. Grandmere's here too. She says I've changed. She says that I seem taller than before.

And you know, maybe I am. She thinks it's because I'm wearing another of Sebastiano's special designs.

Michael and I kissed good night outside my apartment,
with the snow falling all around us.

But I don't think that's the reason. And it isn't love either. Well, not completely.

It's because I feel happy about myself and my life.

I feel like a princess in a story.

A story with a happy ending.

Points for Understanding

1

1 "But now my life isn't ordinary at all." Why does Mia say this?
2 Why isn't Mia happy about having a boyfriend?
3 Why doesn't she want to break up with Kenny?

2

1 Who is Judith Gershner and why is Mia jealous of her?
2 What advice does Mia's father give her about Michael?
3 What does Kenny say that shocks Mia?

3

1 Which two friends does Mia tell about Kenny's phone call? What do they say?
2 Why does Mia feel happy after talking to Tina?
3 Why is Lilly mad with Mrs Spears? What does she plan to do?

4

1 How does Grandmere know that Mia is lying?
2 What advice does Grandmere give Mia about Kenny?
3 What happens in the corridor between lessons?

5

1 What does Lilly say is wrong with Mia's list of boys?
2 What is happening at school on December 18th?
3 What is Mia's plan about Michael? Why does she think it will work?

6

1 How does Mia stop the student walkout?
2 Why does Sebastiano's assistant take photos of Mia?
3 Mr Gianini suspects that Mia turned on the fire alarm. How do
   we know this? Why isn't Mr Gianini angry with her?

7

1 Why does Mia break Lana's cell phone? How does
   Principal Gupta punish her?
2 What does Michael ask Mia in the Instant Message?
3 Why does Mr Gianini buy the Christmas tree?

8

1 Why is Mia jealous of Lilly?
2 Why is Mia's dad angry with Sebastiano?
3 Why does Sebastiano send Mia the dress?

9

1 What surprise does Mia have each morning at school?
2 Why does Sebastiano say Mia has lost him money? How does
   Mia make him change his mind?
3 What is the "Secret Snowflake" game?

10

1 What surprise does Mia get when she turns on the computer?
2 Why does she run to the Girls' Room with Tina?
3 What mistake does Kenny make?

11

1 How does Grandmere make Mia go to the Winter Dance?
2 Who comes to the dance to see Mia?
3 How did Michael know Mia was sending him the cards?

Glossary

1 **algebra** (page 7)
   a type of mathematics that uses letters instead of numbers.

2 **stepfather** (page 7)
   someone's step father is their mother's new husband in a second or later marriage.

3 **pregnant** (page 7)
   if a woman is pregnant, she has a baby growing inside her body.

4 **cancer** (page 8)
   a serious illness caused by the cells in the body spreading in an uncontrolled way.

5 **chemotherapy** (page 8)
   the use of special drugs. It is often used to treat cancer.

6 **heir** (page 8)
   someone who will receive money, property or a title when another person dies.

7 **Dowager** (page 8)
   title of a woman who has money or property because her dead husband belonged to a high social class.

8 **cocktail** (page 8)
   a drink, usually with a lot of alcohol, made by mixing different drinks together.

9 **Thanksgiving Day** (page 9)
   a North American national holiday which takes on the fourth Thursday in November in the U.S. and the second Monday in October in Canada. At *Thanksgiving*, families get together for a traditional meal to celebrate everything they are grateful for.

10 **kidnap** (page 10)
   to take someone away and make them a prisoner, usually because you want their family or government to give you money or make them do what you want.

11 **Emperor** (page 10)
   a man who rules a country or a number of countries.

12 **anonymous** (page 11)
   something that is written by someone whose name is not known.

13 **break up (with)**—*to break up* (with) (page 11)
   to end a relationship or marriage.

14 **ice-rink** (page 12)
a large flat area of ice where people go to *ice-skate*.
15 **project** (page 12)
a piece of work, for example at school, that involves finding out information about a subject.
16 **clone** (page 12)—*to clone*
to create an animal or plant in a laboratory that is an exact copy of another animal or plant, using the original animal or plant's DNA. *DNA* is a chemical in the cells of all living things.
17 **Christmas Eve** (page 14)
the day or evening before *Christmas Day*.
18 **fashion designer** (page 14)
person whose job is to decide the shape and appearance of clothes.
19 **velvet** (page 14)
fabric that is very soft on one side and smooth on the other.
20 **realized** (page 15)– *to realize*
to know something and understand something.
21 **ungrateful** (page 18)
not grateful or thankful to someone who has been good to you or kind to you.
22 **homeroom** (page 19)
a place where students go at the beginning of each school day and the teacher checks which students are not in school
23 **grab**—*to grab* (page 21)
to take hold of something in a rough or rude way.
24 **besides** (page 21)
a word which connects a statement to the statement which came before.
25 **approve of** (page 23)—*to approve of*
if you approve of something, you think it is good or suitable.
26 **protest** (page 23)—*to protest*
if you *protest* against something, you show that you disagree with it and want to complain about it.
27 **nostrils** (page 26)
the two holes at the end of your nose.
28 **carnival** (page 32)
an event held for fun (at a school) in which you can play games for prizes.

29 **booth** (page 32)
   a small enclosed space where you can look at things.
30 **violet** (page 34)
   a small plant with dark purple flowers and a sweet smell.
31 **locker** (page 34)
   a cupboard, for example, at school, where you keep books, clothes and other personal things.
32 **fire alarm** (page 35)
   a piece of equipment that makes a loud noise to warn people that there is a fire and that they must leave the building.
33 **fire drill** (page 36)
   occasion when all the people in a building pretend there is a fire inside and practise getting outside safely.
34 **limousine** (page 37)
   a large, expensive and comfortable car.
35 **suspect** (page 41)—*to suspect*
   believe that someone has done something, usually bad.
36 **crushed** (page 43)—*to crush*
   to hit or press something so hard that you damage or destroy it.
37 **loft** (page 44)
   room at the top of a building, under the roof.
38 **suspend** (page 44)
   to temporarily stop someone from going to school because they have done something wrong.
39 **took place**—*to take place* (page 46)
   to happen, but it is often planned.
40 **model** (page 47)
   person whose job is to show clothes by wearing them at fashion shows or for magazine pictures.
41 **concierge** (page 48)
   person whose job is to look after a building like a hotel and watch people coming in and out.
42 **forgive**—*to forgive* (page 51)
   to decide you will not be angry with someone who has upset you.
43 **press conference** (page 53)
   an official meeting where someone makes a formal statement to journalists.
44 **Greenpeace** (page 53)
   an international organization whose aim is to protect the environment.

45 *snowflake* (page 55)

a single piece of snow that falls from the sky.

46 *printout* (page 56)

a piece of paper printed with information from a computer.

47 *dude* (page 57)

informal way of addressing a man in North America.

48 *make fun* (of) (page 63)—*to make fun* (of)

to make jokes about someone or something in an unkind way

49 *fire escape* (page 64)

a metal staircase on the outside wall of a building that people use to get out when there is a fire inside.

Dictionary extracts adapted from the Macmillan English Dictionary © Bloomsbury Publishing Plc 2002 and © A & C Black Publishers Ltd 2005.

Exercises

Vocabulary: meanings of words from the story

Put the words and phrases in the box next to the correct definitions.

algebra	bodyguard	cancer	cocktail	musician	freshman
flunk	dowager	be sick	heir	traffic	allow	diary
anonymous	artist	ruler	smart	weird		

1		a book in which you write about your experiences every day; a journal
2		a type of mathematics that uses letters instead of numbers
3		someone who makes paintings, sculptures and other works of art
4		a student who is in his or her first year at an American high school or college
5		to fail a test or course in a school
6		a serious illness which is often treated by chemotherapy
7		someone who will receive money or property when a person dies
8		someone who controls a country; a monarch
9		a woman who holds a title such as Queen or Princess from her dead husband
10		a drink, usually with a lot of alcohol, made by mixing other drinks
11		vomit; throw up
12		the vehicles that are traveling in an area at a particular time

13		to give someone permission to do or have something
14		someone who plays music skillfully
15		someone who does not give their name
16		a person whose job is to protect an important person
17		clever; intelligent
18		strange and unusual; a little crazy

Writing: rewrite sentences

Rewrite the sentences using the words and phrases in the previous exercise to replace the underlined words.

> **Example**   My Mum is <u>expecting a baby</u>.
> You write: *My Mum is pregnant.*

1 I'm <u>in my first year at high school</u>.

2 I <u>will inherit my father's title</u>.

3 I heard my mother <u>throwing up</u>.

4 The roads <u>will be very busy</u>.

5 Lars' <u>job is to protect me</u>.

6 Boris <u>plays music a lot</u>.

7 His clothes are <u>really strange and unusual</u>.

8 Judith is much <u>cleverer</u> than me.

9 I <u>failed</u> algebra.

Vocabulary: anagrams

The letters of each word are mixed up. Write the words correctly.
The first one is an example.

Example:	HEROMEPATCHY CHEMOTHERAPY	the use of special drugs to treat cancer
1	POOP FEVAR	think that something is good and suitable
2	ONCLE	to create a copy of an animal or plant from a DNA pattern
3	JORCPET	a piece of written work at school that involves finding out information
4	GLEARNTUFU	not thankful to someone who has been good to you
5	TOPREST	to disagree and complain about something loudly or to take action like marching through the streets
6	SINSTROL	the two holes at the end of your nose
7	PINTTOUR	a piece of paper printed with information from a computer
8	CROPFENCERS SEEN	an official meeting at which someone makes a formal statement to newspaper and TV reporters

9	PUNDESS	to stop someone from going to school because they have done something wrong
10	CROKEL	a cupboard with a key where you keep books and personal things at a school
11	FLOT	a room at the top of a building under the roof

Grammar: complete sentences

Here are notes for Mia's diary. Write them in complete sentences.

> **Example:** Long Island 4 Thnksgving dinner
> You write: *We went to Long Island for Thanksgiving dinner.*

1 left early – traffic bad

2 had 2nd invite to Plaza Htl at 7.30

3 met Sebastiano – fashion designer

4 Kenny askd me 2go2 Big Wong rstnt

5 Lilly making trouble yesterday – sent email abt walkout

6 broke Lana's mobile – suspended 1 day

7 mum said 2 me – you need a vacation

8 will b leaving 4 Genovia tmrw 2 p.m.

Grammar Focus: *besides*

This is a function word. It does not mean *next to* (beside). It is close to *also; in addition to; as well as; other than; as well; too.*

Example:	We study English and other subjects.
A	*Besides English, we study other subjects.*
B	*We study other subjects besides English.*

Write similar sentences.

1	Clean Co. Ltd. makes soap and other household products.
A	
B	

2	The Eiffel Tower is not the only thing to see in Paris.
A	
B	

Another use of *besides* is to give an extra reason or excuse for doing or not doing something. It is close to *in any case.*

Example:	You don't want John to come. You've invited too many people. John isn't a party person.
	I don't want John to come. We've invited too many people already. Besides, John isn't a party person.

Write similar sentences.

3	You don't want to go to the theatre. It's a long way. It's expensive.

4	You don't want to go out tonight. The weather is bad. You have a busy day tomorrow.

Use of words: polite avoidance

In the story, Mia talks about "the L word" meaning LOVE. You hear people talk about "the C word" meaning CANCER because they don't like to say the word itself. Another way of avoiding unpleasant or embarrassing words is to make a negative sentence using an opposite of the unpleasant or embarrassing word.

Match the impolite/too direct to the more polite/less direct sentence. The first one is an example.

	NOT POLITE / TOO DIRECT	MORE POLITE / LESS DIRECT
1	He's very sick (and may die).	A I'm not Lana's favourite person.
2	He's an old man.	B He's not very well (not very well at all).
3	Mia is doing badly at school.	C The food in the cafeteria is not very good.
4	She's stupid.	D Mia is not doing very well at school.
5	Algebra is boring.	E Kenny didn't get the best marks.
6	The food is bad in the cafeteria.	F Lilly isn't the most attractive of girls.
7	Service is slow.	G He's not a young man (any more).
8	Lana hates me.	H Algebra isn't the most interesting of subjects.
9	Kenny got the worst marks.	I Service is not very quick/fast.
10	Lily is ugly.	J I'm afraid she isn't the cleverest of people.

1	2	3	4	5	6	7	8	9	10
B									

Vocabulary Choice: words which are related in meaning

Which word is most closely related? Look at the example and circle the word which is most closely related to the word in bold.

Example: **diary**   milk-product   (journal)   cowshed   illness

1	**ordinary**	normal	unusual	weird	strange
2	**freshman**	clean	liberated	deodorant	student
3	**subject**	citizen	pressure	topic	defeat
4	**extra**	additional	super	ordinary	common
5	**test**	underwear	exam	name	rocket
6	**border**	uninteresting	lodger	plank	boundary
7	**change**	remain	stay	alter	after
8	**ruler**	meter	monarch	minister	party
9	**shocked**	surprised	experiment	lightened	powerful
10	**tired**	attempted	weary	bound	awake
11	**weird**	wonderful	beautiful	strange	caught
12	**semester**	brother	sewing	joker	term
13	**suit**	clothes	set	sugar	candy
14	**join**	accompany	woodwork	team	wedding
15	**fall**	balloon	airy	leaves	autumn

Vocabulary: opposite meanings

Look at the example. Circle the word which is nearest to the opposite meaning.

Example: **everything** all   always   never   (nothing)

1	**smart**	clever	stupid	intelligent	witty
2	**well**	oil	water	ill	wise
3	**final**	first	last	end	eventual
4	**nervous**	scared	brave	calm	afraid
5	**shy**	throw	confident	safe	careful
6	**different**	same	other	also	besides
7	**answer**	reply	letter	question	responsible
8	**terrible**	awful	dreadful	sad	wonderful

Published by Macmillan Heinemann ELT
Between Towns Road, Oxford OX4 3PP
Macmillan Heinemann ELT is an imprint of
Macmillan Publishers Limited
Companies and representatives throughout the world
Heinemann is a registered trademark of Harcourt Education, used under licence.

ISBN 978 0 2300 3750 2
ISBN 978 1 4050 8717 9 (with CD pack)

Illustrated by Karen Donnelly
Cover illustration by Nicola Slater

Printed in Thailand
2010 2009 2008
5 4 3 2 1

with CD pack
2010 2009 2008
7 6 5 4 3